W9-BIF-330

WITHDRAWN

Peer Mediation

Agreeing on Solutions

by Robert Wandberg, PhD

Consultants:
Roberta Brack Kaufman, EdD
Dean, College of Education
Concordia University
St. Paul, Minnesota

Roderick W. Franks, MA
Licensed Psychologist, Certified Mediator
Minneapolis, Minnesota

LifeMatters
an imprint of Capstone Press
Mankato, Minnesota

Thank you to the students of the Hennepin County Home School, who provided valuable feedback for the direction this book has taken.

LifeMatters Books are published by Capstone Press
PO Box 669 • 151 Good Counsel Drive • Mankato, Minnesota 56002
http://www.capstone-press.com

Printed in the United States of America

Library of Congress Cataloging-in-Publication Data
Wandberg, Robert.
      Peer mediation: agreeing on solutions / by Robert Wandberg.
           p.   cm. — (Life skills)
      Includes bibliographical references and index.
      ISBN 0-7368-1023-4
      1. Interpersonal conflict in adolescence—Juvenile literature. 2. Conflict management—Juvenile literature. [1. Conflict management. 2. Interpersonal relations.] I. Title. II. Series.
      BF724.3.I56 W36 2002
      303.6′9—dc21   2001001338
                                                  CIP

Summary: Defines peer mediation in practical terms and shows how it helps people get along. Describes the peer mediation process, including an example of a peer mediation session between two students. Also explains how to move from being a mediator to becoming a mentor.

Staff Credits
Charles Pederson, editor; Adam Lazar, designer and illustrator; Kim Danger, photo researcher

Photo Credits
Cover: ©Tim Yoon
International Stock/©Mark Bolster, 11; ©Patric Ramsey, 17; ©Scott Barrow, 52; ©Stefan Lawrence, 57
Photo Network/©Tom Campbell, 40; ©Esbin-Anderson, 49
Pictor, 20/©Daemmrich, 9; ©Llewellyn, 47
Unicorn/©Bill McMackins, 35
©Tim Yoon, 5, 15, 25, 33, 43, 51
Visuals Unlimited/©Jeff Greenberg, 7; ©Steve Strickland, 27

A 0 9 8 7 6 5 4 3 2 1

Table of Contents

Chapter Overview

Peer mediation is a process for solving problems among people. A neutral mediator helps the students in conflict to create their own solutions.

Peer mediation is not about judging who is right or wrong but is about solving problems.

Conflicts can be internal or external. Peer mediation helps to solve external conflicts. Peer mediation isn't a trial, though. It's different in several ways.

Studies have shown that peer mediation is effective in solving problems among students.

CHAPTER 1

Peer Mediation: A Solution Approach

Have you ever had a problem with another student at school? It may have been name-calling or pushing. It could have been almost anything. How did you solve the situation? Many schools use a particular method to solve such challenges before they become major problems. The method is called peer mediation.

This book introduces you to peer mediation. It's a process that can solve problems before they have a chance to harm students and the entire school. This chapter calls the process **SolutionMatters**. Peer mediation includes seeking healthy options and communicating honestly.

Jack and Ann, Age 13

One day on the school bus, Jack started to tease Ann. The teasing increased until a fight started. The bus driver reported the students to the principal, who called the pair into his office. When the principal asked why they were fighting, they said they really didn't know. The principal said that knowing why wasn't the most important thing. The question was what they were going to do so it didn't happen again.

What Is Peer Mediation?

Jack and Ann had a dispute that they couldn't seem to solve. The principal didn't want to solve the problem for them, but it needed to be fixed. Fortunately, the school had a peer mediation program. The principal had the two students attend a mediation session.

Generally, mediation is an attempt to bring about a settlement between two or more people or groups. Even national governments sometimes use mediation.

In school, students sometimes can't solve their own disputes. In these cases, peer mediation may be helpful. It involves a mediator, who is a trained, neutral third student or trained team. The mediator works to mediate, or bring agreement between two people or groups. A goal of peer mediation is to avoid violence. Another goal is to work out differences in respectful and constructive ways.

Disputes may arise from accidents, such as bumping into someone in a crowded hallway.

By understanding the process, you can increase your knowledge and skills as a critical thinker. You can solve problems better, be more responsible, productive, and self-directed, and communicate better.

Some disputes are accidental. For example, two students bump into each other in the hall, and one believes it was on purpose. Some disputes are intentional. For example, one student calls another names. Peer mediation is often an effective method to achieve an agreeable solution. Students who are involved in peer mediation often learn new ways to handle disputes, disagreements, and conflict. This is true both of the mediators and of the disputants, or students with conflicts.

What Is Conflict?

Conflict is a normal, natural part of everyday life. Often, we consider conflict to be the same thing as violence. Actually, conflict is merely a disagreement. However, having unresolved and lingering conflicts can and frequently does lead to violence.

There are two types of conflict. One type involves personal choices. It's an inner conflict that pushes a person toward solving a problem or making a decision. This is often called an intrapersonal conflict. Mediation usually isn't needed for this kind of conflict. For example, Susan had enough money for only one CD, but she wanted two. She had to decide which one to buy.

The other type of conflict is a dispute between two or more people. Conflict between individuals is often unavoidable. Even in good relationships, no two people can agree on everything. Peer mediation focuses on this second type of conflict.

Conflict may stem from physical characteristics and appearance, intellectual differences, or social or economic status. Perhaps you see conflict in school, on television, or in your community. The more conflict you see, the more acceptable it may become. Many times, the conflict you see, especially on TV or in the movies, has few, if any, consequences. If this occurs, the willingness of people to engage in conflict and violence may increase. As a result, we all suffer.

What Peer Mediation Is Not

Peer mediation is not about discovering who is right and wrong. The students involved in the peer mediation process are encouraged to move beyond their dispute. They learn to figure out how they will get along with each other. The mediators try to create an atmosphere that allows the disputants to tell their stories. Mediators continue to assist the students in identifying ways to resolve the conflict and move toward a positive future.

A peer mediator is not a judge. A mediation session is not like a trial.

Peer mediation also isn't a trial. Peer mediation differs from a trial in four ways. The following chart shows how.

Differences Between a Trial and Peer Mediation

Trial	Peer mediation
Assumes someone is guilty and someone is innocent.	Doesn't assume that someone is guilty or innocent.
Seeks to learn the truth.	Seeks to find a reasonable solution.
Deals with facts.	Deals with the facts and also the feelings behind them.
A judge or jury makes a decision for the disputants.	The disputants themselves make the decisions.

Conflict that leads to violence doesn't affect only adults. About 280,000 U.S. high school students are attacked physically each month. One in five high school students carries a weapon to school. Even in elementary school, students have a 10 percent chance of being regularly bullied.

Peer mediation is designed to help students better understand the nature of conflict. That way, they can begin to see that using violence isn't the only way to respond to conflict. Students can learn skills to solve everyday problems with friends, other students, teachers, parents, and community members.

Student mediators stress the theme of respect. They encourage the disputants to work for an agreement to meet their needs in the best possible way.

Why Peer Mediation?

To deal effectively with conflict, we must learn basic conflict resolution skills and resources. Peer mediation is one resource. Many North American schools have used peer mediation successfully. It provides an alternative to the traditional school system of punishment to resolve conflict. Many students can be trained to become a peer mediator.

Peer mediation is designed to prevent or reduce conflict among students. It can prevent violent or emotional disturbances among students who are in conflict.

Peer mediation is not appropriate for violent disputes or conflicts involving weapons.

What Happens in a Peer Mediation Program?

In peer mediation, mediators help their classmates to identify the problems causing the conflicts and to find solutions. Peer mediation is not about finding who is right or wrong. Instead, it's about moving beyond the immediate conflict and learning how to get along with others. Few things are more important.

Peer mediators ask the students with a conflict to tell their story, and they ask questions for clarification. This usually is positive because the students feel that someone understands their situation. Some students report that just knowing someone understands reduces the tension in a peer mediation session. The mediators then help the students identify ways to solve the conflict.

Some common conflicts are appropriate for peer mediation. These conflicts often involve name-calling, spreading rumors, stealing, boyfriend-girlfriend issues, accidental bumping, and other threatening behavior. Mediation has successfully resolved many student conflicts in these areas.

Not every kind of student problem or dispute is appropriate for peer mediation. For example, sexual or other physical assaults don't go through a school's peer mediation program. Neither would other criminal activities.

Do Peer Mediation Programs Work?

Studies have shown that peer mediation has been effective in resolving 90 percent of elementary school conflicts. The studies suggest that physically aggressive behavior dropped as much as 65 percent because of peer mediation.

Peer mediation often works well because the students in the conflict are empowered during the process. This means that their power to resolve the dispute is recognized. Mediation sets the stage for all disputants to be winners.

The beauty of a peer mediation program is that everyone benefits. Both the students and school staff learn valuable communication and mediation skills. Student mediators often experience increased feelings of self-esteem, authority, and control. The students in conflict benefit by learning to communicate more effectively. They may become more aware of racial and other stereotypes, or oversimplified beliefs about groups of people. Students also learn to deal with conflicts nonviolently.

The word *conflict* comes from the Latin word *conflictus*, which means "striking together."

Points to Consider: SolutionMatters

What is peer mediation?

How does peer mediation differ from other ways of resolving conflict?

What are the differences between peer mediation and a trial?

Give examples of conflicts that aren't appropriate for peer mediation.

Chapter Overview

Peer mediation benefits the disputants and the mediators. It teaches critical thinking, problem solving, responsible citizenship, self-directed learning, and communication skills.

A self-assessment can help you rate your life skills and communication skills.

Peer mediation often is done in teams. These teams use positive peer pressure to solve disputes.

There are many reasons to consider a peer mediation program at your school.

CHAPTER 2

Skills for Interacting With Others

In peer mediation, teens listen, talk about, and together create solutions that resolve disputes. This chapter identifies a number of communication skills and personal characteristics of successful mediators. These **InteractionMatters** can be assets when working through a problem with classmates.

Kris, Age 12

"I got involved with peer mediation in fourth grade. Training sessions taught me how to be a mediator. I found out that mediation is helpful in solving problems.

"Another peer mediator and I sit down with the kids and go over the basic rules. Then, one by one, they tell their story without any interruptions. Either I or the other mediator reviews what we have heard throughout the session. After that, the people involved in the conflict suggest a solution for the problem. The kids decide on a reasonable solution.

"Mediation is a great system. Kids enjoy it more than having to go and talk to the principal about their conflict. The kids I have mediated seem more comfortable talking to people their own age. We are their peers, and they respect us because they know that what we talk about is confidential. I have learned many great problem-solving skills from mediation. The kids I mediate learn ways to solve problems instead of fighting."

Peer mediation can improve the classroom learning that takes place. Students can focus on the subject and not on conflicts.

What Are the Benefits of a Peer Mediation Program?

Many schools have peer mediation programs. Many students of all ages like these programs in their school. Peer mediation provides an alternative to traditional disciplinary practices.

Schools that currently have a peer mediation program report several benefits.

It may help to improve grades. Schools and classrooms that can focus on teaching and learning are more productive.

It promotes positive self-esteem and self-respect in students. This applies to the mediators as well as to the students who are in the middle of a disagreement.

It teaches students skills for interacting with others. The primary purpose of a peer mediation program is to help students resolve their own conflicts and disagreements.

It teaches life skills commonly used in other areas such as sports, jobs, community, and family. Peer mediation programs teach five basic life skills. They are critical thinking, problem solving, responsible and productive citizenship, self-directed learning, and effective communication.

Check yourself for these skills using the self-assessment on the next page.

Read items 1–22 below. On a separate piece of paper, write for each item the number that best describes you. Use this scale:

3 = Almost always   2 = Sometimes   1 = Hardly ever

Critical Thinking and Problem Solving

1. I think about problems and issues on many levels (personal, family, school, and community).	3	2	1
2. I locate current, believable, and appropriate information.	3	2	1
3. I make intelligent decisions.	3	2	1
4. I think creatively.	3	2	1
5. I set short-term goals (less than one year).	3	2	1
6. I set long-term goals (more than one year).	3	2	1

Responsible and Productive Citizenship

7. I contribute to a safe and productive family.	3	2	1
8. I contribute to a safe and productive school.	3	2	1
9. I contribute to a safe and productive community.	3	2	1
10. I take care of myself.	3	2	1
11. I avoid high-risk behaviors such as using alcohol or other drugs.	3	2	1
12. I choose nonviolent ways to deal with problems and conflicts.	3	2	1

Self-Directed Learning

	3	2	1
13. I am good at language arts.	3	2	1
14. I am good at math.	3	2	1
15. I am good at health promotion and disease prevention.	3	2	1
16. I gather, analyze, and apply information.	3	2	1
17. I have good social skills.	3	2	1

Effective Communication

	3	2	1
18. I clearly explain information orally.	3	2	1
19. I clearly explain information in written form.	3	2	1
20. I clearly explain information using a computer.	3	2	1
21. I work for programs, policies, and positions that I feel strongly about.	3	2	1
22. I cooperate with others.	3	2	1

Add up your points. The closer you are to 66 points, the more of these life skills you probably possess. Look at the areas and questions in which you gave yourself a low score. What are some ways you might improve those scores?

Communication is vital in mediating disputes.

Are You a Good Communicator?

The key to successful conflict resolution is communication. Peer mediation helps students learn accurate ways to communicate their ideas and feelings. Teens developed the following self-assessment. It represents their opinion of what's important to think about regarding communication.

How's My Communication?

Read items 1–14 below. On separate paper, write for each item the number that best describes you. Use the following scale:

3 = Almost always   2 = Sometimes   1 = Hardly ever

1. I like to talk with other people.	3	2	1
2. I listen well when others are speaking.	3	2	1
3. I use the Internet to communicate with others.	3	2	1
4. I use the telephone to communicate with others.	3	2	1
5. I can communicate without words.	3	2	1
6. I write letters and notes to my friends.	3	2	1
7. I respect what other people say.	3	2	1
8. I can express my thoughts and feelings to others.	3	2	1
9. I am comfortable when speaking to a group.	3	2	1
10. I like to share my ideas.	3	2	1
11. I encourage others to share their ideas.	3	2	1
12. I ask questions when I need more information.	3	2	1
13. I think before answering a question.	3	2	1
14. I make eye contact when I am speaking to someone.	3	2	1

Peer mediators must be skilled and confident communicators. The closer to 42 points you scored, the better your communication skills probably are. You may want to consider becoming a peer mediator in your school.

QUOTE

"We continue to have success with our peer mediation program. The mediators handle many minor conflicts that otherwise use hours and hours of administrators', teachers', and guidance counselors' time. The peer mediators learn an important skill and build their self-esteem. The disputants learn to handle their conflicts using communication skills they never knew they had! They also observe their peers in a positive role. Everyone wins!"–Ms. Menninger, high school counselor

Peer Mediator Teams

In some schools, peer mediation is successful because it uses peer pressure in positive ways. For example, teams of peer mediators monitor school grounds during times when risk of conflict is high, such as during lunch periods or class passing times.

The mediators are generally introduced to the entire school body at a schoolwide assembly or during schoolwide announcements. That way, everyone is aware of what role the mediators play. Peer mediators are often assigned, if possible, in teams of eight. One pair of mediators is assigned to each quarter of the school grounds at peak activity periods.

Selling a Peer Mediation Program in Your School

If you're trying to promote a peer mediation program in your school, you may wish to tell your teachers, counselors, or administrators this information. A school peer mediation program:

Promotes a safer and more positive school climate.

May result in fewer teacher and administrative disciplinary actions.

Can result in fewer suspensions, detentions, and expulsions.

May improve communication among students, teachers, administrators, and parents.

Nonverbal language is an important part of communication. Nonverbal language, or body language, includes body position, eye contact, or facial expression, for example.

Can reduce violence, property damage, and constant school absenteeism.

Can provide a way for students to resolve conflicts that doesn't require the attention of administrators.

Can resolve conflicts permanently by addressing their causes.

Ask your school administrators to consider peer mediation. It might work at your school.

Points to Consider: InteractionMatters

Suggest some ways to start a peer mediation program in a school.

What are some advantages of having a peer mediation program?

Which of the life skills on pages 18 and 19 is your strongest? Which ones need most improvement? Explain your answers.

Chapter Overview

There are seven steps to follow to have a successful mediation.

The first three steps are to find a time and place, explain the process, and set the ground rules. These steps take place before people begin to tell their story.

The fourth step is to tell the story. During this step, the disputants get to tell their side of what happened.

The last three steps are to think of options, agree on solutions, and end the mediation. The disputants think of realistic ideas, and everyone agrees on a plan for carrying them out.

CHAPTER 3

The Process

During a conflict, thinking clearly is sometimes difficult. The term **MediationMatters** means learning a helpful approach to follow during a dispute resolution. This chapter outlines a step-by-step approach for peer mediation. By following these steps, teens can be heard and begin to identify solutions.

Seven Steps to Success

Peer mediation is serious and should be treated seriously. There are seven specific steps for an effective and successful peer mediation process.

Step 1: Finding the right place and time

Step 2: Explaining the process

Step 3: Setting the ground rules

Step 4: Telling the story

Step 5: Generating options and solutions

Step 6: Gaining resolution and agreement

Step 7: Having closure, departure, and follow-up

TEEN TALK

"I was arguing with this other guy during lunch break. He was calling me names, I was calling him names. Pretty soon, a crowd gathered around. All the kids in the crowd started chanting, 'Fight, fight!' I didn't want to fight, and I don't think the other guy did either. But I felt like I had to, with all the people around. Everyone would have thought I was chicken if I didn't. So we fought. It was a pretty bad time."–Earl, age 15

Step 1: Finding the Right Place and Time

Finding the right spot for mediation is sometimes a challenge. The best place is somewhere away from other people. This helps the disputants to be less distracted or embarrassed. Other students may encourage the disputants to fight. Taking the disputants out of such a situation is extremely important.

Often, a school has a room set up for peer mediations. This may be a classroom or conference room. Sometimes, the school's counseling office sets up a schedule for using the room. It's important that the peer mediation room be quiet and have a door to ensure privacy during the mediation.

At the time of a conflict, tempers may be running high and the disputants may not be prepared for mediation. Allowing them time to cool off a little is sometimes important. The time for the mediation should be convenient for mediators and disputants. The disputants should appear in the room with each other at the same time.

A quiet conference room or office is a good place for peer mediation to take place.

Step 2: Explaining the Process

This step introduces the mediators and the disputants to each other. Generally, all participants introduce themselves.

The peer mediation process is explained during this step. Often at this point, the disputants are nervous. It may be helpful for the mediator to say something like, "Nobody's in trouble. We're just here to talk about a possible problem and to solve it before there's trouble. This is an opportunity to solve the conflict without school disciplinary action or parent involvement."

The mediator must work hard to remain neutral during the mediation process. Both disputants should feel that the mediator values them equally as worthy human beings. Sometimes a reminder is necessary that this is peer mediation, not peer counseling. Peer counseling is more intensive. It involves deeper issues of personality, health, relationships, and so on related to mood or behavior. Peer counseling requires much training.

During the introduction, the mediator explains that the disputing parties will make their own agreement. They must respect each other and be allowed to state their side of the conflict without unnecessary interruption.

Step 3: Setting the Ground Rules

The setting and following of ground rules provides an orderly and respectful peer mediation process. When all parties know what to expect, they can feel more confident in the process.

The mediator is in charge of setting the ground rules. Here are some common ones. All participants are expected to:

Be respectful.

Work hard to solve the problem.

Be as open and truthful as possible.

Express feelings without physical violence or name-calling.

Listen without interrupting while another is talking.

Take responsibility for carrying out the agreement.

Keep the situation confidential.

Keeping the process confidential is critical. When confidentiality isn't maintained, consequences may result. A disputant may be embarrassed. Other students may ridicule the disputants.

There are some exceptions to the confidentiality ground rule. Information about drugs, alcohol, or weapons won't be confidential. Neither will information about child neglect or abuse, or about danger to people. Mediators must tell school staff or administrators when information such as this comes out.

Step 4: Telling the Story

During this step, blame isn't assigned, nor is it decided who is right or wrong in the situation. Disputants have the opportunity to tell their story uninterrupted. The mediators ask the disputants to define the conflict and to express their feelings nonviolently.

It's important that both disputants have an equal opportunity to share their stories. When their stories have been told, the mediator wants to make sure everyone understands the conflict. The mediator attempts to understand the facts and then discusses and summarizes the stories and feelings.

Sometimes, each disputant is asked to pretend to be the other one. When they can "walk in each other's shoes," they may be able to understand and solve the conflict better.

Step 5: Generating Options and Solutions

This step includes the time to work on a solution. The disputants are encouraged to brainstorm their own possible solutions to the problem. Mediators write down all possible solutions. If the disputants run out of ideas, mediators can suggest other options. The disputing students communicate to find a solution that they both agree on. A solution or agreement is not forced upon them. The disputants feel empowered because they are vital in thinking of options and solutions.

Some solutions may surface as wishes during this time. For example, a student may say, "I wish he would quit calling me names."

If the disputants can't think of solutions, the mediators could ask each disputant, "How would you like things to be?" Then the mediators might ask, "What would it take for you to help make that happen?"

In rare instances, the mediator may hold a private meeting with each disputant to get things moving. This meeting often helps disputants with issues involving worry, stress, fear, or personal information.

The mediator describes it as a private, confidential discussion with each disputant while the other disputant waits outside. The mediator asks if the disputants would agree to try it. The mediator promises confidentiality during the meeting. But if helpful information is suggested, the mediator tries to find a way in which the disputant would be comfortable in sharing it. If not, the mediator shouldn't force it! Both disputants should be in their private meeting for about the same amount of time before the group mediation restarts.

Step 6: Gaining Resolution and Agreement

Once the options are generated, everyone agrees on one to try. When agreement is reached, the mediator writes a contract describing what each student agrees to do. The disputants sign it. Sometimes the contract can be verbal. Whether written or verbal, the contract should be in the disputants' own words. The key points of the agreement are:

The disputants create it.

The disputants consider it to be reasonable.

It describes future behaviors and possible timelines.

The disputants can reasonably achieve it.

Aimee, Age 13, and Juliana, Age 14

Aimee had been having problems with Juliana, another girl in science class. Their problems became so bad that their teacher suggested mediation. Among the solutions suggested was for the girls to work together on a science project. That way, they'd get to know each other better. The two girls still aren't friends, but at least they're more friendly toward each other. Both agree that mediation worked well for them.

Step 7: Having Closure, Departure, and Follow-Up

The final step in the peer mediation process is closure of the peer mediation meeting. The mediator alerts the disputants that other students may want them to continue their dispute. Sometimes, the mediator suggests further discussions if there's a need to check the progress of the agreement.

The disputants are thanked for using mediation. They also are thanked for working together to settle their conflict and for letting the mediation service help them. The disputants typically return to class.

Points to Consider: Mediation Matters

Why do you think it's important to be away from other students during mediation?

If you were a peer mediator, which of the seven steps do you think would be the most difficult? Explain.

Name some exceptions to the confidentiality rule.

Chapter Overview

Two students, James and Markus, have a problem that calls for peer mediation.

Jerica, a peer mediator, helps Markus and James follow the seven mediation steps.

James and Markus solve their problem successfully. They hope to improve their relationship with each other.

CHAPTER 4

Mediation in Action

In this chapter, you'll watch a morning in the life of two students, Markus and James. You'll see how the peer mediation approach works at their school. Not all mediation processes are the same, because each conflict is different. The people involved are unique. This chapter's **StoryMatters** can help you apply what you've learned to your own situation.

Remember that Chapter 3 described the steps for a mediation. They are:

Step 1: Finding the right place and time

Step 2: Explaining the process

Step 3: Setting the ground rules

Step 4: Telling the story

Step 5: Generating options and solutions

Step 6: Gaining resolution and agreement

Step 7: Having closure, departure, and follow-up

In this chapter, you'll use the mediation process to practice the steps. Periodically, you'll pause to reflect on the action.

The Scene

Markus is a regular high school student. During the past couple of months, he's shot up in height. He's now taller than his father. This makes him feel clumsy, but he's managed to survive so far. He gets decent grades and recently got a part-time job at the restaurant down the block. He's planning to save money for a car.

Today, he gets up and gets ready for the day with a quick shower and a glance in the mirror. Things look okay. He rummages around for his favorite jeans, a shirt, and sneakers. A light splash of cologne, a deep breath, and he feels more confident. Breakfast is usually a couple of pieces of toast with peanut butter and a few swallows of orange juice. His mom checks him over, asks about homework and his plans for after school, then gives the okay. Then it's out the door to meet the bus.

On the bus, there's talk about last night's game and the math assignment that's due later. At school, the kids head off down the hall.

The hallway is busy. Markus opens his locker door. He pulls out the books that he needs for the morning and sets them on the floor behind him. He bends over to put his backpack into the locker.

Even tripping over your shoes can be a potential cause of conflict.

Within seconds, he is headfirst in his locker. His books are scattered across the floor to the other side of the hall. Markus recovers to see James stumbling behind him. A few people are laughing. Others act surprised.

Question: Do you think this was an accident or intentional?

Markus doesn't trust James. He thinks about grabbing James but decides against it. Instead, he yells, "You did that on purpose, man!"

"It was an accident. I wouldn't touch you on purpose even if you paid me," James hollers back.

"You're always picking on me and then saying that it wasn't your fault," accuses Markus.

"I can't help it if you're falling down all the time."

Mr. Jones, the assistant principal, arrives. "See you guys in my office, now." Neither boy has physically attacked the other. Except for acting surprised or laughing, no other students are involved. Mr. Jones is thankful no serious violation of school rules has occurred.

Question: Does this situation call for peer mediation? Why or why not?

"My idea of an agreeable person is a person who agrees with me."–Benjamin Disraeli, British writer and politician

Step 1: Finding the Right Place and Time

Mr. Jones calls Ms. Wong, the adviser of the school's peer mediation team. Then he escorts Markus and James next door to the conference room. This is a neutral location that's quiet and out of the way.

Mr. Jones says, "Rather than my suspending you, it helps when someone your own age can listen to your stories. Ms. Wong said she's sending a peer mediator now to discuss the situation. We'll just wait here until the mediator comes. It's convenient and private, so others can't overhear what you say. Too bad we don't have somewhere with comfortable chairs and a table. We have used the counselor's office, the lunchroom, and the library. But those places aren't as good because other students and staff use them during their free time."

Question: Why does Mr. Jones want a quiet, private place for peer mediation?

Step 2: Explaining the Process

Jerica, a classmate of Markus and James, walks in. Mr. Jones introduces her as a trained peer mediator.

Jerica sits down and says, "I'm not here to solve your problem. I am here to help you think of your own solutions. Each of you gets a chance to talk without being interrupted. My job is to listen without taking sides. Whatever you say will be confidential, unless you're involved in something really unhealthy.

"We're going to brainstorm ideas about dealing with the problem. Then we'll set a time to get back together to see if it's working. We're scheduled for a half hour here. Usually that's enough time. If we need more, I'll talk to Ms. Wong and schedule another time and place to meet. Any questions? Is there any reason that either of you doesn't want me as your peer mediator? If there is, then let's talk about it now."

Markus and James look at each other, then at Jerica. They both know her and respect her, but neither boy is really a friend of hers. Neither teen has any objections.

Question: Might your best friend have trouble mediating for you if you had a problem with another student? Why or why not?

Step 3: Setting the Ground Rules

"Let's begin with the ground rules," says Jerica. "These rules help us to build trust and to work together to solve the problem. They help people know that what they say is important and that they'll be heard."

The three of them agree on the following:

Don't interrupt the other person.

Don't call each other names.

Don't grab each other or use other physical aggression.

Tell the truth.

Question: Could there have been other ground rules in this situation? What might they have been?

The Federal Bureau of Investigation (FBI) noted that almost 60,000 hate crimes were reported in the 1990s. Hate crimes are based on prejudices against other people.

Step 4: Telling the Story

Jerica says, "Now let's talk about what happened. Markus, why don't you start?"

Markus says, "I was standing by my locker. My books were behind me, and James pushed me into the locker."

James tells his story, "I was walking with my buddies. The hall was crowded, and I tripped on Markus's books. I accidentally bumped him, and he fell into the locker."

Jerica asks, "Anything else?"

Markus says, "This isn't the first time that James has bumped or pushed me. It seems like too much of a coincidence to always be an accident. I used to brush it off, but now it makes me angry."

Question: Should the peer mediator care whether the bump was an accident or intentional? Explain.

Step 5: Generating Options and Solutions

Jerica says, "It's time for us to think of possible solutions. To begin with, we won't judge or eliminate any of them. I'll just write them all down. Markus, let's list your ideas to keep the two of you from bumping into each other. After you're done, James gets his chance." Markus and James tell Jerica their ideas.

Question: Why is it important to list all possible solutions, even ones that don't seem workable?

Together, Markus and James come up with the following suggestions:

Stay out of the hallway when the other person is there.

Give Markus a bodyguard.

Assign a different locker to one of the boys.

Say "hi" every morning and then walk away.

Work together on a school service project so they get to know each other better.

Get different shoes that aren't so clumsy.

Take walking lessons.

"Anything else?" asks Jerica. The boys shake their head. "Now, rate the items. Number your first choice as one, second choice as two, and so on. Don't skip any. Our goal is to choose a solution that you both will try and that you think will resolve the problem."

James and Markus were able to shake hands at the end of their mediation.

In numbering their choices, Jerica asks them to think about the following:

Is the choice reasonable?

Did you say it just because it was funny?

Can it be easily done?

What's the cost?

Can we do it in our school setting?

What are the advantages?

What are the disadvantages?

Questions: How would you rate the ideas? Could the boys have thought of other ideas? If so, what?

After discussing each item, both boys decide that they don't know each other well. James admits that he's been prejudiced against Markus. They agree to say "hi" each morning and then walk away.

Questions: Have you ever had problems with another student because of cultural, racial, gender, religious, or ability differences? If so, what happened? Did you overcome the differences? How?

Step 6: Gaining Resolution and Agreement

"How will saying 'hi' and walking away solve the problem?" asks Jerica.

James says that he won't be tempted to pick on Markus if he knows him better. Markus says that he won't accuse James of picking on him if they can talk without being aggressive. That may help them build a friendlier relationship.

Question: What else could Markus and James do after they say "hi" to each other?

Step 7: Having Closure, Departure, and Follow-Up

"Let's fill out a contract," says Jerica. "You both write what you've agreed to do. I'll include all the suggestions we talked about. Then we all sign the contract."

After filling out the contract, Markus and James decide to meet with Jerica in a week. Both sign the contract, get a copy, and shake hands as they leave for class.

"See you guys next Tuesday at eight here in the conference room!" Jerica signs the contract, too, and takes it to Ms. Wong.

Points to Consider: StoryMatters

Have Markus and James benefited by this experience? Why or why not?

Was Jerica a good peer mediator? Why or why not?

What do you think might have happened between Markus and James if the school didn't have a peer mediation program? Why?

Chapter Overview

Some people have to be mediators even when they haven't had special training. It is possible to do so with a little practice.

There are several guidelines to follow as an informal mediator. They are to guide, not judge; stay neutral; meet in person; and set the mood.

Active listening is essential to help mediate a dispute.

Just relax and do your best.

CHAPTER 5

✿

Suddenly, You Are a Peer Mediator!

Have you ever been in the middle of a disagreement between two of your friends? You don't disagree with either friend but feel forced to calm the storm between them. This situation seems to happen frequently during the teen years.

Maybe you haven't been trained in peer mediation, but you still can help to find a solution. In this chapter, **PeerMatters** helps you realistically assess your mediation skills. You might find that you have strengths to build on or areas you'd like to learn more about. You can use mediation skills, even without special training as a mediator.

Lawrence, Janette, and Clark, Age 14

Lawrence walked into first-hour class, and there stood his friends Clark and Janette, arguing hotly. "Hey, what's going on, you guys?" asked Lawrence. His friends started to tell him how wrong the other person was. Clark looked at Lawrence and said, "Why don't you tell us who's right?" Lawrence could see that both his friends expected him to support them. He'd never been in this situation before and didn't quite know what to do.

Important Guidelines

Lawrence had never had the chance to be trained in peer mediation, but he wished he had been. Like Lawrence, perhaps you've been asked to help solve a disagreement. Even if you never have received formal training as a mediator, you can still follow some guidelines.

Guide, Don't Judge

As a mediator, you're not a judge and jury but rather a guide and assistant. You don't force a solution on the disputants. Mediators offer few suggestions or opinions. The disputants are responsible for developing their own solutions to the problem. Skilled mediators help disputants see their problem and explore options to resolve it in a way that everyone can accept.

Communication is never one-sided. It involves not only sending messages that others can understand but also understanding the messages that others send.

Stay Neutral

Staying neutral takes some practice. Read the following three situations and answer the questions.

Joe, Theresa, and Maria, Age 16

1. Joe pours milk down Mike's back in the lunchroom because Mike picked on Joe's younger brother at the bus stop.

2. Theresa wants to date Tanya's boyfriend. Theresa is worried because she's heard that Tanya is going to beat her up after school.

3. Maria and Darren are screaming and swearing at each other in English class.

Questions:

1. Who do you think is at fault, Joe or Mike? Explain.

2. Did Tanya or Theresa do anything wrong? Explain.

3. Who do you suppose started yelling first, Maria or Darren? Explain.

The correct answer to all three questions is, "I don't know." You don't have enough information to judge. If you immediately took sides, you violated a critical part of being a peer mediator. Peer mediators must remain neutral!

TEEN TALK

"Aleesha and Jane used to be good friends. But I guess Aleesha and another girl were having a fight about a boyfriend. They asked Jane to help them figure it out. Without hardly thinking, Jane said Aleesha was wrong. I don't think that's what the two girls were looking for. Anyway, Aleesha won't even talk to Jane anymore."–Carla, age 14

With friends involved, staying neutral is often difficult. This can be tough, but it is essential. It becomes easy to encourage one friend to bend more toward a resolution than the other friend. To be a true mediator, you must demonstrate complete neutrality in the dispute. Neither friend should feel less valued in the peer mediation process.

Staying neutral means watching your body language and the amount of eye contact with each friend. It means avoiding any behavior that may show a preference for one friend over the other. Remaining neutral is one of the most difficult tasks of a peer mediator.

Face to Face

Face-to-face communication is essential. Attempting to mediate by telephone, letter, or e-mail is not recommended. Direct communication, often at an intense feeling level, is an important element of peer mediation.

The process may start with your friends seemingly telling on each other to you. However, your task as the peer mediator is to get your friends facing and talking directly to each other. Have the disputants direct their statements toward each other. For example, imagine one says, "I don't know why he is picking on me." You could simply say, "That person is here. Go ahead and ask him."

Remaining neutral is important for peer mediators. A neutral facial expression is helpful.

Set the Mood of the Meeting

The mood and atmosphere are important ingredients in a successful mediation. The peer mediation should occur in a climate of trust, safety, and confidentiality. With the right approach, you can guide your friends to let down their guard and argue their viewpoints respectfully. Ultimately, you want your friends to work together to solve their dispute.

Issues should be stated with respectful words and in neutral terms. For example, imagine the disputants are calling each other "pig" or "idiot." You will have to ask them to be more respectful.

Ask one disputant to begin talking about the problem. Things can get heated here. That's okay, as long as everyone obeys the ground rules.

Listen!

Draw out emotions and ideas with active listening techniques. To hold an effective conversation, your listening skills need to be top-notch.

Listening is much more than just hearing the words. It involves sending and receiving messages. For example, don't just think about what you're going to say and not hear the other person. Listening skills include body language, eye contact, and appropriate questions.

Pay attention to the words and body language of each speaker. Don't do something else when someone is trying to speak to you. That can be annoying. As you speak, pay attention to the reactions of your listeners. Watch and listen for signals that tell they have understood your message.

Be sure to encourage the disputants as they talk. This is an important part of listening. When people feel someone is listening, they are more likely to be open about their feelings. This will help everyone find a solution.

Relax!

You may become a mediator for your friends. By applying the information in this chapter, you'll be able to be successful. Just relax and do your best.

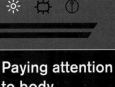

Paying attention to body language and encouraging others are both part of listening.

Points to Consider: PeerMatters

Describe a time when you were called on to act as a peer mediator. How did you feel?

What does "guide, not judge" mean?

Why do you think face-to-face communication is recommended over other forms of communication during peer mediation?

How might teens become better communicators?

Chapter Overview

Getting help from other people is a way to show your commitment to growth. A self-assessment can help you understand yourself in order to grow.

The mentor survey can help you see if you have the potential to be a mentor yourself.

Prejudice consists of feelings against individuals or groups based on stereotypes. Discrimination is acting on those prejudices.

By being a mentor or mediator, you can help yourself and others positively deal with prejudice and discrimination. Many ideas can help you be a mentor or mediator.

CHAPTER 6

☼

From Mediator
to Mentor

This chapter introduces **MentoringMatters**. It's about recognizing skills that you want to develop and identifying other people who may assist you. It's also about being a mentor for others. A mentor is a person who can serve as a model and can guide and support you. In this chapter, you'll see that you can be both a mentor and someone who has a mentor.

As you have read, peer mediation involves others in your life and problems. Like a solid friendship, the process takes time, patience, risk, and a lot of trust. By discussing your situation calmly with another person, you can learn from your emotions. You may define a conflict, focus on solutions, and change negative behaviors or attitudes.

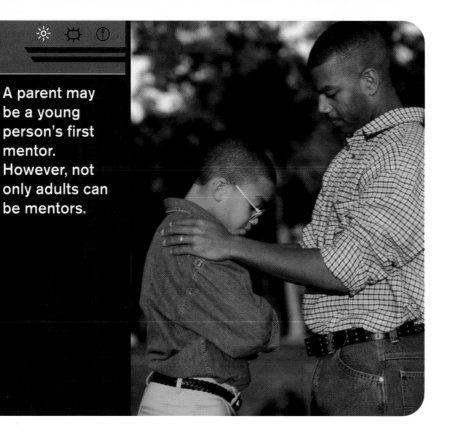

A parent may be a young person's first mentor. However, not only adults can be mentors.

Getting Help From Others

You occasionally may need assistance to talk about differences, listen to others, negotiate, or mediate a compromise. Perhaps you've come to understand that asking for help is a sign of maturity rather than weakness. A mentor can guide you in understanding or support you in a new way of doing things.

You have the power to change and grow. Finding the right people to assist you with new behaviors makes a powerful statement of your commitment to growth. Finding a mentor may seem like a small step. As the saying goes, "A journey of a thousand miles must begin with a single step." To use peer mediation, or to be a mediator or mentor yourself, takes a desire to understand yourself.

Look at the following self-assessment. It contains items that may help you understand yourself.

Read items 1–18 below. On a separate sheet of paper, write for each item the number that best describes you. Use this scale:

3 = Almost always   2 = Sometimes   1 = Hardly ever

1. I speak confidently about my ideas.	3	2	1
2. I share concerns about myself without being fearful.	3	2	1
3. I identify my goals.	3	2	1
4. I work on new skills.	3	2	1
5. I change bad habits.	3	2	1
6. I meet new people.	3	2	1
7. I think positively.	3	2	1
8. I ask for other people's opinions or help.	3	2	1
9. I listen carefully.	3	2	1
10. I control my temper.	3	2	1
11. I express concern for others.	3	2	1
12. I care about other people's feelings.	3	2	1
13. I identify my strengths.	3	2	1
14. I challenge myself to try new things.	3	2	1
15. I motivate others.	3	2	1
16. I see opportunity in failure.	3	2	1
17. I make time to relax.	3	2	1
18. I use resources to help make good decisions.	3	2	1

The closer your score is to 54, the more you value and possess skills important in peer mediation and mentoring.

The Mentor Survey

Mentors are often adults, but not always. They may be people with experiences that you value. They may have skills or knowledge that you want to learn. They are genuinely interested in you and want you to be successful.

Are you wondering whether you could be a mentor? Take this quick survey to find out your mentoring potential.

Can I Be a Mentor?

Read items 1–12 below. On a separate piece of paper, write for each item the number that best describes you. Use this scale:

3 = Almost always   2 = Sometimes   1 = Almost never

1. I care about what happens at school.	3	2	1
2. People talk with me about their worries, frustrations, and concerns.	3	2	1
3. In conversations, I spend more time listening than talking.	3	2	1
4. Other people help me recognize hidden abilities.	3	2	1
5. I have received a quote or saying that has influenced my thinking or behavior.	3	2	1
6. Others have helped me to learn about how things work or how to get things done.	3	2	1
7. I've been encouraged to find a way to deal with challenges in life, in activities, or at school.	3	2	1

The word *mentor* is very old. A story is told that a man of ancient Greece, Odysseus, sailed off to war. His servant and friend, Mentor, promised to teach Odysseus's son, Telemachus, how civilized people should behave. Odysseus was gone for years, yet Mentor kept his promise. Thanks to Mentor, Telemachus turned out to be brave, honest, and respectable.

8. I receive the right help at just the right time.	3	2	1
9. I know people who've helped me to grow and strengthen my character.	3	2	1
10. I know someone who inspired me to shift the direction of my life positively and constructively.	3	2	1
11. I reach out to people who are deeply in need.	3	2	1
12. I observe, read, or experience things that have a positive effect on my strengths and abilities.	3	2	1

The highest possible score is 36. The higher your score, the more likely you've experienced the positive influence of others. Also, the more you probably appreciate and respect the effect that you can have on others.

DID YOU KNOW?

The word *prejudice* comes from the word *prejudge*, which means "to make a judgment without information."

Using Diversity in Mentoring

Of the billions of people in the world, no one else is like you, not even your family members. Even identical twins are different from each other. The people of North America are very diverse. We come in all shapes, colors, and sizes. We represent a wide variety of world history, religion, race, and culture. Our diversity makes for creative, interesting, and exciting moments.

What Are Prejudice and Discrimination?

Diversity can lead to misunderstandings and confusion among people. Words and actions sometimes may separate people rather than bring them together.

Sometimes people have negative feelings such as suspicion or hatred for individuals or groups. The name for these negative feelings is prejudice. This is often the result of stereotyping. For example, you may dislike someone because the person goes to a different school. You stereotype everyone from the school as unlikable, even though that's not the case. It's like saying all blue cars refuse to start on cold days.

Today's world is growing more diverse. It's important to understand that everyone—even twins—are unique individuals.

Prejudice often results from lack of understanding and can lead to fear. This fear sometimes leads people to commit hate crimes, which often include physical attacks and property damage. Age, religion, race, or sexual orientation are often the basis of hate crimes.

Many terms associated with prejudice end in the letters -ism. *Ageism* is prejudice against people in any age group, young or old. *Sexism* is prejudice against people based on their gender. *Racism* is prejudice against people of certain races or cultures.

Discrimination is acting on a prejudice. It can involve avoiding, excluding, or verbally or physically abusing someone. Unfortunately, prejudice and discrimination are all around us. We often see examples in books and on TV.

Respecting Differences

Prejudice and discrimination may lead to conflict, which may call for mediation. As a peer mediator or mentor, you must learn to respect the diversity around you. You can work to avoid prejudice and discrimination. Here are 15 quick ideas.

Learn to count to 10 in five different languages.

Point out that all people are different, unique, and special.

Challenge stereotypes. Avoid making or laughing at discriminatory jokes or comments.

Encourage people to feel good about themselves.

Avoid hurtful words.

Respect others and cooperate and work with all people.

Read books that show diverse people.

Learn about holiday customs in different cultures.

Empathize with others' feelings.

Don't buy toys, videos, CDs, or other products that reinforce stereotypes.

Attend various cultural concerts and other events.

Watch travel videos about other countries.

Join a pen pal organization.

Learn about the music and art of different countries.

Get to know people from other cultures and backgrounds.

Have you already done any of these? How many could you do within the next month?

ten dez dieci kymmenen ti tio juu diez on zece sepuluh ashara tien de'ka zehn

Even learning to count to 10 in another language can help to reduce prejudice and increase understanding among people.

Words to Live By

Here are some thoughts from writer Rebecca Barlow Jordan. See how they apply to your life: "It's not how many goals you reach, but how many lives you touch . . . You can make a difference in your world."

Points to Consider: MentoringMatters

What is a mentor? Do you think you could be a mentor? Explain.

How can jokes contribute to prejudice?

What antidiscriminatory actions do you believe are most difficult for teens? Why?

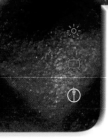

NOTE

At publication, all resources listed here were accurate and appropriate to the topics covered in this book. Addresses and phone numbers may change. When visiting Internet sites and links, use good judgment. Remember, never give personal information over the Internet.

Internet Sites

Big Brothers Big Sisters of America
www.bbbsa.org
Youth mentoring organization, with links to find local groups

National Committee to Prevent Child Abuse
www.childabuse.org
Information and statistics related to child abuse, as well as violence prevention tips

Hot Lines

National Youth Crisis Hot Line
800-448-4663
Short-term counseling for teens in conflict

Useful Addresses

Family Service America
11700 West Lake Park Drive
Milwaukee, WI 53224
1-800-221-2681
www.fsanet.org
Help for resolving family and other problems

Office of Victims of Crime Resource Center
PO Box 6000
Rockville, MD 20849-6000
1-800-627-6872
www.ncjrs.org
Resources for victims of conflict

National Organization for Victim Assistance
(NOVA)
1757 Park Road Northwest
Washington, DC 20010
1-800-879-6682
www.try-nova.org
Provides assistance for victims and survivors of
conflict

Southern Poverty Law Center (SPLC)
400 Washington Avenue
Montgomery, AL 36014
www.splcenter.org
Includes ideas on opposing hatred and
prejudice for individuals, schools, and
communities, plus links to other hate watch
groups

For Further Reading

Lantieri, Linda, Janet Patti, and Marian Wright Edelman. *Waging Peace in Our Schools.*
    Boston: Beacon, 1998.

MacBeth, Fiona. *Playing With Fire: Creative Conflict Resolution for Young Adults.*
    North Kingston, RI: New Society, 1995.

Teolis, Beth. *Ready-to-Use Self-Esteem and Conflict-Solving Activities for Grades 4–8.*
    Paramus, NJ: Center for Applied Research in Education, 1995.

Wandberg, Robert. *Conflict Resolution: Communication, Cooperation, Compromise.*
    Mankato, MN: Capstone, 2001.

Wandberg, Robert. *Tolerance: Celebrating Differences.* Mankato, MN: Capstone, 2002.

Glossary

compromise (KOM-pruh-mize)—to reach a solution through give and take

confidentiality (kon-fuh-den-shee-AL-uh-tee)—privacy

dispute (diss-PYOOT)—a conflict that involves at least two people

empower (em-POW-ur)—to recognize the power a person has in resolving conflicts

facilitate (fuh-SIL-uh-tate)—to assist

ground rules (GROUND ROOLZ)—statements that all individuals agree on in peer mediation; ground rules set the foundation for settling a conflict.

mediation (mee-dee-AY-shuhn)—a process of settlement or compromise between people, groups, or nations

mediator (MEE-dee-ay-tur)—a person who helps individuals or groups reach a settlement or compromise in a conflict

mentor (MEN-tor)—a person who has skills, knowledge, or characteristics that another person values and wishes to learn

neutral (NOO-truhl)—not taking sides

peer (PEER)—a person who is about the same age as another

prejudice (PREJ-uh-diss)—negative attitude toward an individual, group, or race of people

stereotype (STER-ee-oh-tipe)—an oversimplified belief about a person or group of people

violate (VYE-uh-late)—to break or abuse a rule

Index

Index Continued